No-Nonsense Practical Guide to Fundraising for Non-Profits

How to Raise Money for Your Charitable Cause

By

Aaron Sanders

Copyrighted Material

Copyright © Autumn Leaf Publishing Press, 2020

Email: Publisher@AutumnLeafPub@gmail.com

All Rights Reserved.

Without limiting the rights under the copyright laws, no part of this publication may be reproduced, stored in or introduced into a retrieval system, or transmitted, in any form or by any means (electronic, mechanical, photocopying, recording or otherwise), without the prior written consent of the publisher of this book.

Autumn Leaf Publishing Press publishes its books and guides in a variety of electronic and print formats, Some content that appears in print may not be available in electronic format, and vice versa.

Design & Illustration by Laura King

First Edition

Contents

Introduction 8

What is Charity? 11

    Two Types of Charity 12

        Christian Charity 12

        Non-Christian or Secular Charity 12

    A Discussion of Charity 13

    Are We an Altruistic Society? 15

What Constitutes a Non-Profit Organization? 21

    The World's Top 5 Biggest Charities 23

        Bill & Melinda Gates Foundation 23

        Stichting INGKA Foundation 23

        The Wellcome Trust 24

        Howard Hughes Medical Institute 24

        Ford Foundation 24

A Brief Look at the History of Charity 26

Music as Charity 32

    Live Aid 1985 34

    Leading Music Charities 36

        Save the Music Foundation 36

        Americans for the Arts 37

    Fender Music Foundation 37

    Other Charitable Efforts 38

A Word About Food 40

A Word About Propriety 42

Charitable Trusts 45

    Two Categories of Trusts 47

        Charitable Remainder Trusts 47

        Charitable Lead Trusts 48

    The Upside of Trusts 48

The Feel-Good Factor 50

Fundraising Ideas to Solve Problems 53

    Think Like a Business 55

        Have a Plan 56

        Consider Technology 56

    Advertise Like a Business Would 57

        Local Radio Stations 57

        Local Publications 58

    Public Access Television and Local TV Stations 58

    Community Center and Programs 59

    Elicit Help from the Chamber of Commerce 59

    Utilize Local Influencers 60

- Be Focused 60
- Online Presence 62
  - Branding is Everything 63
  - The Mission Statement 64
  - About Page/Defining Yourself 64
  - Online Donations 65
- Open an Organization Shop 66
  - Legalities 67
  - Day to Day Working 69
  - Be Up to Date 69
- Online Help 71
- Planning an Event 74
  - Establishing an Entity as a Charity 76
- Hiring a Publicity Company 83
  - How to Find the Right Event Planner 84
  - Pros of Hiring a Pro 86
- Plan a Lottery or Raffle 87
  - What Makes a Lottery? 88
- Other Local Fundraising Ideas 90
  - Selling Vintage Clothing 93
  - Craft Sales 94

- Car Wash 94
- Go to the Dogs 94
- Host Special Nights 95
- Community Yard Sale 95
- Babysitting 96

Faith-Based Fundraising Ideas 97
- Prayer Meetings 102
- Pop-Up Café 103
- Spiritual Concerts 103
- Donation Boxes 103
- Bake Sale 103
- Auctions 103
- Carol Singing 104
- Work-a-thon 104
- Dinner Event 104
- Crowdfunding 105
- Email Fundraising 106

School Fundraising Ideas 108
- Kindergarten/Pre-school 110
- Elementary Schools 111
- High School 111

University 112

Corporate Fundraising Ideas 114

Fundraising in General 120

Why People Do Not Donate 124

Conclusion 127

Resources 130

*"No one is useless in this world who lightens
the burdens of another."*
Charles Dickens – English Author

Introduction

All non-profit organizations rely on volunteers to help them function; for many, they are the backbone of the organization. In most cases, their limited funds prevent them from hiring talent, so they need it. The expertise of the unpaid helps them to survive.

For five years, I volunteered at a local homeless shelter. I had wanted to give something back to the community by helping others. It was a community charity partly funded by grants and sponsorship events. It is a sad fact that sometimes while working in these situations that the people who are meant to be the caregivers, are in fact, more in need of help than those they are caring for.

Part of the job was dealing with those who have a diverse range of immediate needs, such as getting thrown out of their house, to those with drug and alcohol abuse, domestic issues, legal problems, and acts of random violence. They also taught English in the shelter for those who were learning it as a second language. This included people from Poland, Pakistan, Libya, and Lithuania to all points East and West of the world. I did a bit of all of these chores, which certainly gave me a headache by the end of the day.

Looking back, I found it, on the whole, a very worthwhile experience. I should warn you. You do eventually run out of patience. Compassion fatigue kicks in, and you eventually burn out; it happens to even the most dedicated supporter all the time of any given charity.

This book is a general look at non-profit organizations. Details will differ wherever in the world you are reading this. Please check local legalities and constraints in your country of origin.

No matter how well you get along with someone in a caring situation, you should never share your address or telephone numbers with them – it only leads to trouble. I speak from a number of very painful experiences. Believe me, you do not want the 3 am wake-up call or the unwanted knock at the door.

"As the purse is emptied, the heart is filled."
Victor Hugo – French Poet and Novelist

What is Charity?

There is a great statement that we are all taught as a child. It is said that "charity begins at home." In reality, that is rarely the case. Charity, by its name and certainly its nature is a fickle beast indeed.

The definition of the word charity is that it is an organization set up to both help and raise money for those in need. They are classed as non-profit making organizations, meaning that once all the day to day running costs of the business are met, all monies left over are for the cause, which is the obvious reason the charity was established in the first place.

Two Types of Charity

Charity is broken down into two categories.

Christian Charity

It is one of the tenants of the Christian faith, part of the seven virtues – humility, chastity, diligence, patience, kindness, and temperance -that cement the ideas behind belief, no matter the church you worship under. Believed to be the most excellent of virtues, it is the habit of charity extended not only to the worship and love of God but the well-being and care of your neighbor. Obviously, it is one of the cornerstones of the Bible and Christian teaching, which should be universally acknowledged by all. Christian charities are exactly that, connected in some way to the good works carried out by the world-wide communities connected with Christianity.

Non-Christian or Secular Charity

The non-Christian charity is basically everything and everyone else. Non-Christian charities are not in any way atheist; it is simply that they are secular and not aligned nor tied to any particular religious group. Neither can they be classified as nondenominational or not tied to a particular faith or religious group. One example is The American Red Cross or The Red Crescent, the Arabic equivalent, which has an open policy to treat all in exactly the same way. As an international body, they have a duty of care to treat everyone, no matter the religious belief, the color of skin, or enemy or foe. There is no judgment of the situation the individual finds themselves in, only help where or when it is needed.

I hope that it is also noted that each religious denomination has its own charitable institutions set up under the principles of their own religion. They, too, have the same duty of care to those that support them and must always be accountable for the actions they take.

A Discussion of Charity

The Jewish religion Tzedakah, which literally means righteousness, is commonly referred to as acts of charity. To do what is right and just is extremely important to the community that money, time, resources to the needy, and generous acts are seen to be done by believers. The Torah requires that 10% of Jewish income be given to a charitable cause, and it is totally irrelevant whether the recipient of these 'righteous deeds' be rich or poor.

In Islam, there are two forms of charity, the first Zakat, which is one of the five pillars on which the faith is based. It requires the believer to give 2.5% of their earnings to good causes in each calendar year. The donation is fixed by the religious authorities and often by a Sharia Court decree. The second is Sadaqa, which is a voluntary contribution. It is simply an act of kindness. It does not require money, time, or anything that will affect your pocket; it may be as simple as smiling at someone.

Charity in the religions of the Hindus and Buddhists is called Dana, which is roughly translated as the virtue and generosity of giving. In fact, it is viewed as disposing of a part of the things you own to a recipient or recipients, without expecting anything in return. It is tied with spiritualism and the eternal search for earthly perfection, the selfless act of going to the assistance of someone in need, and alleviating that need no matter the cost to oneself. It can also take on the invisible form of philanthropic public projects in order to empower and help the actions of the many rather than the few. It can also be viewed as almost a spiritual release, an act of letting go, of cleansing the soul and spirit in readiness for the next set of challenges that will beset your life. Though the best charity is the giving of the soul, that selfless belief that to give part of yourself and your time is far better than the giving of money.

Charity, in its purest form, is an act of giving of oneself, whether it be time, money, or goods for the benefit of those less well-off, or who may be destitute. This charity should be extended to beggars, the homeless, those who are elderly, living alone, or are in some way in need of assistance. It can be a religious act, such as the giving of alms.

The tradition of Maundy Money is a UK tradition of giving to the poor during Holy Week by the Monarch themselves, dating back to the time of Henry VI, or the washing of the feet of the poor and the giving of alms on the same day by the Pope. Of course, it is the outward showing of virtue, the act of being seen to do good, rather than just the doing of it.

Again, it can be viewed that Charity should concentrate on one's own immediate group, our friends or family, known as filial piety, as opposed to cold charity. Charity without affection, which is in the name of help, is given to everyone else. But no matter the name or cause, charity is the giving of the basic necessities of life: food, water, healthcare, clothing, shelter. It is about unjust imprisonment, and the rights of those incarcerated, social injustice, political prisoners, world poverty, the plight of orphans, and endangered species. The list is endless, and certainly too many to be listed here. It is about just about every reliable – and in some cases unreliable - cause you can think of.

Are We an Altruistic Society?

It is the first duty of every government on Earth, no matter the political society it presides over, to provide its people with certain necessities. At their most basic, they include schools, healthcare, policing, and an effective army. They also include a basic duty of care to provide a working infrastructure that supports, nourishes, and enhances the lives of its citizens.

Also, these responsibilities are not acts of charity, they are simple rudimentary needs. The government should not be raising up the strong to be stronger and forgetting the weak.

It was one thought that Communism, which grew from the writings of Karl Marx, was the answer to everyone's problems. We would all live in a worker's paradise, a classless utopia provided by the State where everything and everyone was equal. But those who implemented the dream, Lenin and Stalin, were no fewer despots than the Romanov dynasty that they replaced, and in some ways far worse. It is a wonderful fairy tale that everyone in society should be equal, a story we may believe will work when we are a child, but as an adult, in the realities of life, we know that it doesn't.

The great problem with 'isms' is that they don't work. All of them fall over themselves and fail. Capitalism. Communism. Socialism. Imperialism. They fail because they refuse to bathe in the understanding that each strata of society has its own needs.

I won't list the differences between the four. That is not the purpose of this book. But it is easy to understand that each has failings. Yes, everyone living under the capitalist system would like to be wildly successful, but in a lot of cases, it is just not possible. They cannot keep up, compete in the cut-throat world of business, or have the chances provided by a favored birth, or the benefit of a good education.

Likewise, under communism, we are not all equal. By the very nature of human existence, we all do not want the same thing. Some are achievers who will want to stride ahead of the crowds and be successful. Some will be plodders, happy with the hand that life has dealt them. While still others will be so confused with the situation, they find themselves in that they barely get off the starting block and simply give up; so, you cannot treat everyone the same.

It should seem obvious that altruism is a social and philosophical movement using the twin strands of logic and the very act of reasoning, in order to find the best and most effective ways of helping others. In theory, it should be about effective impact. That is to say that those who are acting on the information have done so after thorough research and investigation. It is about prioritizing a system of ongoing research to

(a) utilize the use of money raised in order to assist the greater good of all
(b) encourage scientific and medical research that can best save or enhance the quality of lives
(c) to promote anything of value that can alleviate the suffering of those who are ill-equipped to help themselves

That is pretty basic and logical stuff to anyone and everyone, except governments, it would seem. It is obvious that in most instances, governments are aware that they are failing their population and that it is to the utter shame of the politicians who are supposed to serve the people who elected them and not the government that they have an allegiance to that they fail so spectacularly. Forgetting, of course, the mantra, "Government for any, by the people." Ignoring or failing to implement policy issues which can save lives and certainly enhance its longer-term quality, which is altruism at its finest, or at least should be!

People may be altruistic, looking out for one another for the common good of the things they hold close to their hearts.

Unless you live in a dictatorship, governments are elected for a fixed term, and most politicians have that fixed-term mentality. They will certainly say anything in order to get elected. Once in that position, they will have no trouble in saying that their political manifesto was not legally binding and that it was only a set of ideas, rather than a set of firm pledges, and of course, the first to suffer are those at their most vulnerable. Go back on a deal, tell a bigger lie - all will get you into the power of the office.

So, I hear you ask, "What is an act of charity for the ordinary individual?" It is a complex one that says a lot about the bigger picture and the unanswered questions of life. We never quite realize that we need someone until we really need them. Bereavement, marital crisis, childbirth are all things that will happen to all of us. These life events, along with death and taxes, are inevitabilities in human existence. Even within the lives of an average couple, they will have acts of altruism. In most healthy relationships, there is a certain fluidity in each other's roles. At some point, one partner is the alpha, another point the other is the alpha.

It is basic parent psychology that overlaps throughout our lives: one minute, we are the parent, the next the child. It is compassion, love for others, and empathy for the situation that they may find themselves in.

Of course, the greatest act of altruism is that of a parent for their child or children. Parents will often subsume their own wants and desires in order to see that their offspring reach their own greatest potential – especially if they show a particular talent.

The opposite of these positive behaviors is the negative ones of selfishness, smugness, and self-satisfaction, which by ignoring the needs of others make us less the sort of people that we want or need it to be.

In extreme circumstances are those who devote themselves to the calling of the priesthood. It is a life of celibacy and complete contemplation on the needs of others. They put their own self wants aside and dedicate their whole existence to the pastoral cares of the flock you look after. By their very nature, the medical profession, social services, teachers, the police, and army are all in the same broad category, in a calling to serve others rather than simply a job.

The care for others is not only found in humans; it is also observed in the animal kingdom with increasing frequency as well. All species show various emotions in nursing a child, adoption of an orphan, help for the sick and injured, and even mourning rituals for the dead. These are all seemingly human characteristics.

This sums up the everyday doctrine of altruism. The main factor is attachment - the ability for an individual to reach out and form a meaningful bond with another human. This leads to veneration - a feeling of deep and profound feeling for someone or something. This leads to goodness - generosity and kindness and a state of moral excellence in the search for being good.

So, to answer the question, yes, we are probably at heart an altruistic society, but only when it suits us. This is ultimately why we have charities.

> *"No one has ever become poor by giving."*
> Anne Frank – Diarist and Holocaust Victim

What Constitutes a Non-Profit Organization?

If you believe recent statistics that there are over one and a half million non-profit organizations registered in the United States alone. It does not take a mathematical genius to multiply that by the number of countries in the world to realize exactly how many charitable concerns there are, and every one of them needs monetary donations.

It is quite probably impossible to calculate the total amounts given to charity every year around the world in whatever form. Take into consideration all the structures involved in keeping the charity active and the well-oiled machinery that keeps it all moving. The personnel, the offices, the pool cars, the daily facts, and accounting figures, not to mention all those expenses, foreign trips, and hotel bills to pay.

The whole point of a non-profit is that they do not do that. The money they do make keeps them afloat, so it stands to reason that they are set on generating as much income they can in whatever way they can to fuel their mission.

Establishing a business of any kind incurs costs. While running the operation, you will have legitimate business expenses. For a non-profit, from there on in, every cent or penny you make legally belongs to benefit those you set the charity up for in the first place. Charities rely on income from donations, from individuals and foundations, corporate sponsorship, government funding, merchandising, grants, and trusts.

The World's Top 5 Biggest Charities

It is estimated that well over $500 billion is donated to charity each year around the globe. Here is a list of the top 5 biggest charities on Earth.

Bill & Melinda Gates Foundation

It's strange to say that at number 1 is the founder of Microsoft with a pot of $37.4 billion. Its projects include the Cambridge Scholarship, the New Schools venture fund, Washington State Achievers Scholarship, The Discovery Institute, and a much wider program of sponsorship and general help. They are also associated with Global Health, Global Development, and other US programs.

Stichting INGKA Foundation

This is the world's largest stand-alone foundation, supporting and promoting innovation in the creative fields of architecture and interior design. It is the owner of INGKA Holding, which deals in furniture such as beds, chairs, desks, and the like. It promotes products that are essentially eco-friendly in design and production. The endowment of Stichting INGKA Foundation is in the region of $36.0 billion.

The Wellcome Trust

Established in 1936 by Sir Henry Wellcome, its headquarters is based in London, concentrating on human and animal health. They are engaged in research on influenza, mitochondrial diseases, human fertilization, and embryology. Its endowment is $22.1 billion, and their other fields of research include understanding the brain, fighting infectious diseases, genetics, and genomic innovation.

Howard Hughes Medical Institute

Mr. Hughes established this non-profit medical research institute with annual investment in biomedical research, amounting to some $825 million. It provides grants to individuals as well as institutions and provides great support to scientific research in the US. In the past, it has funded Nobel Laureates like Thomas Steitz (chemistry), Jack Szostak (physiology or medicine), Craig Mello (physiology or medicine), amongst others. It also funds several other research programs.

Ford Foundation

This foundation was created in 1936 by the Ford brothers, Edsel and Henry, as a private foundation. Its programs include a contribution to arts, education, and development, especially in the third world. The foundation deals with wide-ranging issues like democracy, rights and justice, education, sexuality, and reproductive health and rights. Its regions include Latin America, North America, India, Nepal, and Southern Africa. This New York-based foundation is a big player in the field of grants for projects, planning, individuals, and grants to organizations that are all looking for sources of funding.

What can we learn from these major charities? Non-profit organizations can span the globe and reach a wide range of needs. They can begin with a wide variety of missions in mind. Where a need must be addressed, a charity can be formed to meet that need.

"For it is in giving that we receive."
St. Francis of Assisi – Friar

A Brief Look at the History of Charity

    2,500 years before the birth of Christ, the Jewish nation instigated charitable giving by the rich to the poor. The word "philanthropy" was first used by the poet and philosopher Plato 2,000 years later, and certainly, by the time of Christ, the Romans were regularly seeing to the basic needs of the millions of poor and starving subjugated under their heel.

Feudalism, which stemmed later, was a hierarchical society. The king at the top, followed by the barons and earls, knights, merchants, and the impoverished poor at the foot of the table. Even when dining at the Lords' great Hall, if you were "below the salt," you were not worth the trouble of anything worthy of respect.

You lived in a shack, and your land, owned by someone else, was laid out under a strip field pattern. They observed high-days and holidays and followed the Christian calendar taught to them by their betters.

In this state of feudalism, no one deviated from the furrow, secure as they were in the knowledge that they bathed in the righteousness of the Lords above, the king, and those who governed them. No one ever traveled more than 30 miles from the village they were born in.

Charity came in two ways

(a) From the influence and largess of the Church
(b) From the forming of Chantry Chapels and monies left by the rich in their wills.

Remember that the church was everything in Medieval Society. It was a law set in place in a lot of European Countries that every one of the population not only went to church each Sunday but observed each Saints day. You could certainly be imprisoned, or worse, if you did not comply.

The whole point of having an existence on earth was to prepare you for the one you were sure to have – as long as you played the game – after death. It was a rock-solid belief that the better you did here, the less time you would spend in purgatory and then be accepted into the life of bliss that lay beyond the golden gates of heaven.

Judaism and the Muslim Faith are all-encompassing religious beliefs that measure out your day from sunrise until sunset. Before the 16th Century, it was the same in Europe. There was only one Christian religion, which was the Catholic faith with the Pope at its head and its bishops and priests carrying out his dictates – with a little help from God himself, of course.

The church was the main outlet for any form of charity. Its very ethos at the heart of many of its religious orders such as the Franciscans, Dominicans, Benedictine, Cistercians, and Augustinians, all of which dispensed alms to the poor and care to the sick.

The Knights Templar and those of St John were mainly involved in martial and medicinal pursuits. Those orders that were mainly closed composed of a life of prayer and contemplation were all that was expected, did the most good for the immediate society, and the charitable work that went on.

The rich founded hospitals for the sick, the infirmed, and especially extensive charitable work with lepers. They also ensured the safe passage of their own spirits through the afterlife by building Chantry Chapels, where prayers were said day and night for the easement of their souls. The poor of the parish were also endowed with daily stipends and financial assistance for a set period of time.

All charitable concerns through the church ended abruptly with the Reformation. All thought of charity and helping the poor and sick was dispensed with under the harsh dictates of many of the monarchs of European kingdoms.

Charity organizations and charitable giving as we recognize it today began in the US in 1732. A French seaman who had been nursed as he was dying in a New Orleans refuge left his not inconsiderable fortune for the use of the city's poor. A hospital and then a charitable foundation were established. Since then, the model for Charity Hospital in the city has been used throughout the world.

So, throughout the last 300 years, during wars, we knitted socks and mittens, we wrapped relief parcels and sent them off to our boys at the front. Knowing, of course, that if the intended recipient was already dead by the time they were received, there was always someone else who could use them.

After the second world war, charitable giving and its skillful collection came on in leaps and bounds, transforming itself from a haphazard way of obtaining money and goods for all those in need, to the well-oiled machine it has become today.

Originally, charity was a direct response medium in which eager organizations turned into what has become the all-purpose charitable model. This is a sort of one size fits all of online giving and direct donor response. Originally, a charity could expect the donor to give directly, and they passed it on to the receiver. Then through some middleman organizations you give to them, they give to the charity, and the charity gives to the receiver.

The US, in particular, has led the way in the bigger picture projects like Donors Choose, which concentrates on a wide range of charitable concerns within the country itself. It is now all about global structures, micro-financing, and individual projects, assessing needs, and giving to those areas of the global society that need it most. They are at the forefront of global giving, dedicated to the welfare of the poor.

The origins of charity, like the origins of original sin, lie in the teachings of the Catholic church, with its very foundation built on the teachings of Jesus Christ himself. The idea of charity comes from the old English language, set to mean a "Christian love of your fellow man." It can be found in the old French word *charité*, which is 12th century in origin. It is founded in the meaning of mercy and compassion, from the Latin word *caritatem*, whose literal meaning is esteemed and affected. It is supposed to signify an intent to help those who temporarily or in the longer term cannot help themselves.

"The best way to find yourself is to lose yourself in the service of others."
Mahatma Karamchand Gandhi -Indian Political and Religious Leader

Music as Charity

Music is one of the great unifiers, it is like a smile, it says so much with so little effort, and is completely universal. Apart from the language barrier, if lyrics are used, it is the combined configuration of the sound of notes that say so much. It is a producer of extreme feelings that can raise up or sink down all who hear it and has been since the dawn of time the rage maker and gift-giver of extreme feelings and the emotions they bring with them.

If there is one thing that raises the awareness of most human beings, it is that of the starving and in particular the starving faces of women and children in abject agony - the gaunt, hollowed eyes, the extended bellies of the terminally hungry and the blank stares of those close to death. These harrowing images were brought home one October night in 1984 by the BBC reporter and newsreader Michael Buerk. Africa, no stranger to famine, was in trouble again, this time, the crops in Ethiopia had failed, and millions were at risk. Two UK musicians, Bob Geldof and Midge Ure wanted to act quickly and do something to help alleviate the problem.

Quickly, they wrote a song, grabbed a gaggle of their celebrity friends, and recorded a single hoping to raise a few thousand dollars the cause. The song, "Do they know it's Christmas Time at all" – Feed the World, was an enormous hit throughout large swathes of the planet. It raised an estimated $10 million, eliciting a swift response by musicians from the US who challenged with, "We are the World." Again, an enormous global hit with an estimated $44 million raised.

It is fair to say that the ex-Beatle George Harrison set up the template for music's involvement with charity after the terrible floods and famine in the Bangladesh region of East Pakistan in 1969. Of course, it was no help that the country was in the throes of a brutal civil war, leading to the deaths of tens of thousands.

His friend, the virtuoso sitar player Ravi Shankar, called him to ask if he knew any scheme that would, in some way, alleviate some of the problems that the region was having. Harrison came up with the concept of the Concert for Bangladesh at Madison Square Garden in New York during August of 1970. Of course, the concerts and the subsequent movie and the success of the accompanying album made it a worldwide triumph. Money poured in, plaudits loaded up, and then the situation was lost to the failings of mankind.

State corruption, tribal corruption, and certainly local government corruption were apparent. By the time the final sums were calculated and were given to those that needed it, it was far less than the considerable amounts that were raised in the first place.

Live Aid 1985

I was there in London on Saturday, July 13th, 1985. I was right in the middle of this sweltering mass of humanity. It was a day of universal joining in a great cause, it was a moment in time when you felt that the whole world was joined together in a common cause to alleviate the suffering of so many tortured souls.

The grand event began in Wembley Stadium in London and ended 18 hours later in Philadelphia. The last performer on the bill in the US was the great wordsmith Bob Dylan, who made a heartfelt plea for a similar concert be put into place to alleviate problems caused by mortgage debt for the US farming community. Hence, Farm Aid was born, and the first concert put on just over 2 months later. It can be looked upon as one of those rare charities that, with the help of musical luminaries like Willie Nelson, Neil Young, and John Mellencamp, have, with a little help from their many musical friends, been a consistent force for good. An estimated $125 million was raised.

Unfortunately, the problem was underestimated – as most funding concerns are – and the $9 million that was raised was woefully short of what was actually needed. You certainly can raise your hat to Messer, Nelson, Young, and Mellencamp, who have arranged and performed concerts practically every year since. So far, in its 34-year history, it has raised $57 million in aid.

It was also startling that in July 2005, Bob Geldof had another go and staged Live 8, a series of concerts in 11 countries to raise awareness of global poverty. He was immensely shrewd scheduling the concerts before the G summits were held. It was not billed as a fundraiser, although some 3 billion people watched the concerts around the world. It was not money he wanted; it was voices raised in protest. The subsequent spotlight forced delegates attending to cancel the entire debt of 18 of the world's poorest nations, make drugs to combat AIDS far more accessible, and double the levels of aid given to those African nations who needed it the most.

Young people should be encouraged to learn to play an instrument – any instrument. They promote positive thinking, encourage outside interest, ward off depression, and above all, promote a life-long friendship.

Therefore, it is sad that within the confines of the American public school system, more than 5 million students have no access to music education at all. Whether that is because of lack of instruments or teachers, or general indifference to the future of the arts.

Leading Music Charities

The three of the leading American Music Charities are as follows:

Save the Music Foundation

This foundation donates instruments, computers, and software to help students, schools, and whole communities more forward through the gift of being able to make music. They believe strongly that music aids in personal development, self-confidence, and learning skills. Having helped over 2,000 elementary and high schools alike, they dig deep and foster the potential for their children.

Americans for the Arts

With offices in Washington and New York, this organization is committed to raising the profile, promoting, and sustaining the arts movement as a whole. It encourages arts and education to thrive in more vibrant and creative communities. It generates private and public sector policies that build individual and community awareness of the power of the arts in all its forms while ensuring financial stability. It allows the organization to follow up on creative opportunities and challenges.

Fender Music Foundation

This is a purely non-profit organization relying on public donations and the selling of music memorabilia. An offshoot of Leo Fender's guitar manufacturing company, its aim is to make playing music accessible for everyone. Its mission statement says it all.

> *The Fender Music Foundation believes that music participation is an essential element in the fabric of an enduring society. Our mission is to have the benefits of making music available to everyone in the communities in which we serve, to promote its importance through education and media initiatives, and to provide financial and in-kind resources in collaboration with other organizations to achieve our common goal.*

Other Charitable Efforts

Cat Stevens, now Yusef Islam, donated all rights to his interpretation of the song *Morning Has Broken* off his third album to the Great Ormond Street Children's Hospital in Central London. Elton John has his own Aids Charity. The Edge and Bono from U2 aligned themselves with the Fender Foundation and have brought in millions of dollars for the cause. Herb Alpert, trumpeter and co-owner of A&M Records, has given over $10 million over the years, and along with countless other music celebrities continue to do so.

Perhaps the pursuit of music and its obvious benefits to the community is an avenue you could go down as a source of revenue for your non-profit organization. Even if you do not play, sing or write yourself, they are many in your community who do.

Look at your local schools. How are they stocked in traditional instruments? Maybe they could do with a makeover - brass, woodwinds, and strings. Or perhaps your school needs guitars, bass, and drums for the more band-orientated pupils. Go to a local music shop and barter a deal for a quantity of good acoustic guitars and a couple of nylon strings for the more classically minded pupils. What about a new organ or grand piano for one or more of your local churches? Put on a concert, or a series of them, with some local talent. Produce a CD comprised of different combinations of local talent playing either their own compositions.

Take over your local radio station for a sponsored block of your favorite artists.

Why not put on a play or a musical? Not only does it get your immediate group involved, but there are also lots of added advantages. Sell the props, the costumes, signed programs, and posters – anything, in fact that is going to make you money. What about a sponsored dinner with the cast, or auction off the best seats in the house? The possibilities are endless!

Music is certainly a good way in which to involve your community and your congregation at large in the wider scope of fundraising. No matter what you do as long as it is organized and executed well, it should bring in returns.

A Word About Food

If we think of the millions of for-profit food companies that exist across the world, that is anything from supermarkets to fast-food restaurants, farmers, and bulk sellers. How much of that unconsumed food is wasted each and every day?

If you feel comfortable fitting into the niche, perhaps the food distribution angle is the one you should follow with your newly set-up charity. Look to all the food outlets in your community to not only use as a drop off point for collection boxes. Think of used clothes or anything that is, in fact, reusable. Collect and sell all of it as a profit for the organization.

You could set up a food bank, eliciting donations from the congregation, which, although worthy, is only a short-term problem in need of a longer-term solution. You could set up an agency to find work, or at least offer temporary employment, to those in need. You could act as a go-between in many ways as the spiritual leader of your congregation.

In the US, many universities have food drives. College campuses actively look for ways that they can utilize excess food in their area. Of course, most of this is dry, canned, non-perishable items that can be stored for distribution.

I found a quote regarding the use of food banks, which is actually uncredited, so I could not give the source, although its message worked rather well in the context of this section.

> *"Rather than acting as a service to ensure people do not face destitution, the evidence suggests that for people on the very lowest incomes ... the poor functioning on welfare can actually push people into a tide of bills, debts and, ultimately, lead them to a food bank. People are falling through the cracks in a system not made to hold them. What little support available is primarily offered by the third sector, whose work is laudable, but cannot be a substitute for a real, nationwide safety net."*

Poverty is not a lifestyle choice; it is a fact of living every day. Sure, there are a lot of people who will actively pursue a chaotic lifestyle, but not many. Most of us want stability and regularity in our existence. If your government cannot rise up to the challenge of feeding its own people, perhaps you can?

"Never doubt that a small group of thoughtful, committed citizens can change the world; indeed, it's the only thing that ever has."
Margaret Mead, American Anthropologist

A Word About Propriety

All charities, as are all individuals, are responsible for their own actions. Because all non-profit organizations are heavily regulated, the utmost honesty and open-handedness are expected in all your dealings.

It is a recognized fact that both large and small charity concerns have more than doubled their worldwide donations in the past 20 years. There is now something like 2.3 million of the organizations registered around the world.

Unfortunately, with a lot of the recent problems of charities, the major concerns are fighting off a lot of very bad publicity. Being a charitable concern, you are there to help, advise, and take care, not to exploit, harass, and sexually abuse, so please remember the following.

Like all good businesses, your charity needs a very strong administrative team at its heart. You need a logical, process-driven, highly organized structure to move things along.

You are a people-centric business. You, your employees, and your volunteers are the backbone of the organization and are crucial to your ultimate success. You should be aware of both their short and long-term development and take a keen interest in their training and well-being.

You must raise awareness of the charity in the hopes that as many people donate and involve themselves as fully possible. You can do this by publicity, marketing, and any form of visual or aural communication, which is essential.

You must be fully aware of your transparency. You can be accused of fakery or misspending donations or using monies donated for your own personal needs. Simply point accusers to the IRS and the Attorney General for your State, who will most certainly put any doubters right.

The non-profit sector is benefitting greatly from the effects of social media, as it enables fast, effective targeting of potential donors, volunteers, and contributors for fundraising and other campaigns aimed at internet users.

Charities need to raise their awareness. Part of this is providing the research, insights, and analysis required to influence the debate. If you are large enough, employ a Grant Officer who will work with the fundraising departments to contribute towards the overall fundraising targets and ensure its long-term sustainability. They will produce high-value, successful applications to new and current US and international trusts and statutory funders and, if required, produce documentation to help do this.

Of course, every charity is structured a little differently, but almost all of them, no matter how big or small, require experts. These could be scientific researchers, lawyers, human rights specialists, and so on. If you're interested in a particular area, you might look at gaining the required training you need first and then move across to the charity sector when the time is right. It's an equally valuable route - and potentially a better one if you want to build up a particular area of expertise.

"No act of kindness, no matter how small, is ever wasted."
Aesop – Ancient Greek Poet

Charitable Trusts

Believe it or not, there is no actual definition of what constitutes a charitable trust. The best you will get is that trusts and foundations are charities with a private, independent, and certainly, a sustainable source that sources out individuals or other organizations to finance.

In brief, what is defined as a charitable trust is usually a set of liquid assets that a donor in particular signs over to beneficiaries to create that foundation. All assets are then held and managed for a period of time with all, or some, as specified, interest going to the cause. It is either in the form of a particular amount, an annuity, or as a unitrust, calculating annual payments on a percent of the value of the trust in any given year.

A charitable trust is a set of assets, usually liquid, that a donor signs over or uses to create a charitable foundation. The assets are held and managed by the charity for a specified period of time, with some or all interest that the assets produce going to the charity.

If you are a huge corporation or certainly an individual who has been very successful in life, they are a great way of getting rid of some taxable obligations, spreading around a bit of goodwill, and certainly doing you no harm whatsoever in the PR stakes. Take a look at the late Elizabeth Taylor's AIDS Foundation or the workings of Sir Elton John.

In the UK, the Peabody Trust was established in 1862 by a US banker to better the housing conditions of the working-class poor. Today, over 160 years later, they control the 55,000 of the social housing available, especially in inner London.

The Joseph Rowntree Trust, currently valued at $24 billion, is now divested into numerous branches. It was set up in 1904 by the famous chocolate family to alleviate the living conditions of the poverty-stricken poor of London.

One should also add praise to Andrew Carnegie, the steel, railroad, and industrial magnate. His greatest act of philanthropism was to establish more than 3,000 libraries in the UK, the US, and Canada for the advancement of knowledge for all, and his supreme efforts to bring education to the masses. They are only two of the many working trusts that have changed the face of modern charitable giving, focusing on everything from poverty to medical advancement.

Two Categories of Trusts

In the US, the guiding force behind charitable trusts is the desire by the wealthy to leave a legacy to all. As in the UK, they can have lots of tax benefits for all concerned. These trusts are divided into two working categories:

Charitable Remainder Trusts

Charitable Remainder Trusts are set up by the owner of the trust in order to provide an income stream, while the charity or private foundation receives the overall value of the trust once it ceases to operate.

Charitable Lead Trusts

Charitable lead trusts are the flip side of the coin. They make payments to the chosen charity for the fixed term of the trust, and on its closure, the donors or their heirs will receive the full value.

It comes as no surprise that the most profitable trusts have grown out of and are based in America. They include the J Paul Getty, the WK Kellogg, the Bloomberg, Robert Bosch, and Mastercard Foundations. In the United Kingdom, there are only two of note, the Garfield Weston Foundation and the Church Commissioners for England.

The Upside of Trusts

So, why set up a charitable trust besides the heart-warming spirit of giving? Tax breaks! Charitable trusts are a win-win both for charities, which receive much-needed funding, and donors, who can access otherwise unavailable tax breaks. For example, highly appreciated assets like stocks are especially vulnerable to enormous capital gains and estate taxes, but under charitable lead trusts, donors can get an immediate federal income tax deduction based on the trust's value. Afterward, income tax is only paid on the revenue the property produces. Once the trust expires and passes to the donor's heirs, estate and gift taxes are substantially reduced.

Of course, while phenomenal tax breaks are one reason to start a charitable trust, some of the largest and most influential private charitable organizations in the world were founded as charitable trusts. For instance, the J. Paul Getty Trust, which is worth more than $10 billion, funds arts programs all over the world, as well as the famous Getty Museum in Los Angeles. Look at the Guggenheim Foundation and the work it does in Venice and engaged in an enormously diverse range of projects in high-poverty areas of the world. The late Jim Henson's Sesame Street and the marvelous Muppets have been funded by the Pew Charitable Trusts and MacArthur Foundations, which have been funding innovative programs such as the Ken Burns series on the Public Broadcasting System in the United States for decades.

"Wealth is not to feed our egos but to feed the hungry and to help people help themselves."
Andrew Carnegie – Businessman and Philanthropist

The Feel-Good Factor

The advent of television has been both a boon and a curse to the charity/non-profit sector. It was in the US that they were first introduced. It was a strange correlation between an intense marketing strategy, combined with brand awareness and building the corporate image that led to their immense success.

Primetime exposure for your brand supporting a good cause was akin to striking advertising gold. All across the country, add-execs and TV execs were putting their heads together and finding new ways to get a brand into bed with a suitable candidate good cause, one that would promote the brand to the optimum, never mind the obvious benefit of tax breaks or loads of free advertising. They seemed to be the instant answer to all the fundraising needs that a non-profit organization might require, while also satisfying the needs of huge corporations.

For two hours of prime-time TV, they could show that they cared deeply enough about a particular cause to spend time promoting it and raising money for it. Hundreds of millions of dollars are now raised this way all around the world for every good cause known to man each year.

I did a little exercise and watched just one hour straight of broadcasting on a commercial station. At that time, there were four commercial breaks, which aired five separate commercials each time. Of that total of twenty commercials, eight were from registered charity appeals.

That means that every single day on the 350+ commercial TV channels, almost 200 appeals for help go out. Multiply that number by all the TV Station that beam into every home 24 hours a day, 7 days a week, 52 weeks a year, there many people with their hand out. With all of those charities appealing for the dollar in your pocket, it is no wonder that commercial stations air so many commercials that rely on advertising as their main source of revenue.

It is not like voting, where no one apart from you knows who you put your X against. It is not a matter of being in church, and the collection plate comes around, and you can be seen to make your donation large or small. It is not even a matter of who you are going to give your hard-earned cash to.

It is for you to ask yourself, am I doing this because I want to? Am I doing this because society expects me to, or is it all just for the ego and satisfaction, the smugness of the thought that thank God – or whoever you turn your inner thoughts toward - it is not you?

I found a great quote on the net, that sums up the cynicism that now surrounds the work of a lot of charities - but could find no attribution to who actually said it – so apologies for that.

> *When confronted with the starving child, we are told: "For the price of a couple of cappuccinos, you can save her life,!" while the true message is: "For the price of a couple of cappuccinos, you can continue in your ignorant and pleasurable life, not only not feeling any guilt, but even feeling good for having participated in the struggle against suffering."*

"Think of giving not as a duty but as a privilege."
John D. Rockefeller Jr - US Business Magnate and Social Philanthropist

Fundraising Ideas to Solve Problems

It is safe to say if you believe the most recent figures, that only 20% of the world's non-profit organizations don't use fundraisers to achieve their charitable aims. That tells you that they have a steady stream of income so that they do not have to stoop so low as to beg. For the rest of them, it is just the hard graft of entrepreneurship and ideas that keep them afloat.

Say you had a favorite house in the community where you lived, which still held some historical value. It was a derelict shell yet had tons of character. You and a few like-minded friends wanted to preserve and restore it to its former glory. One way you could garner support for this venture would be to start a non-profit organization and raise funds to save it.

Perhaps you live in an area where there are lots of neglected or stray animals. You could save them either on your own or with the help of others by forming a non-profit organization. This way, you can partner together with others who have the same passion.

There is an old boat beached by the harbor wall, it was historically important as it carries 100 years of history in its rotting frame. You could repair and restore if you set up a non-profit organization to do so.

There is a child distressingly in need of medical care in your community. Your church roof needs repair. A playground needs to be re-vamped. A sports field needs a makeover. You know your community and its needs. You can establish a non-profit organization to fix it.

It is all about enthusiasm. It's amazing how getting together with a few friends soon turns into a wider coffee morning, then into a public meeting. Enthusiasm sells, and that is what you are doing. You are selling the idea of helping others so that they indeed can, in the long run, help themselves.

Your non-profit must be about your passion. You must believe in the cause deeply because you are going to give it a lot of time, effort, and energy. You have to give it everything you have. You can achieve and do anything if you really want to. If you have the motivation, the determination, the drive, and the self-will to achieve it.

Think Like a Business

Have a goal in mind. Choose different methods of fundraising. Identify the purpose of it all. It is about identifying the need in your market, building a bridge from one to the other. How it is going to be now and, in the future, building long-term relationships and long-term brand loyalty.

If you are competing in a particular market, you must have the edge over your competitor. Your product, for example, might be fighting hunger in your neighborhood. Rather than selling an actual tangible good, you are selling altruism. In this process, think like a business. You must be better than any other charity that has the same goal in mind. State your case better than them. Be better than them! It is the only way to get money into your bank account.

Have a Plan

A good way to start the fundraiser process is by setting a goal. The goal is the amount of money that needs to be earned for the fundraiser. This amount might not be achieved, but it helps to know what to aim for, and if it is lower than you expected, there may be some way you can adjust that by other means.

You should evaluate the audience you are targeting; one cause will attract more attention than another. If it is your local community, you should be looking at what is needed. Charities need not be all major global concerns. If you are going to get involved, then the only way you will succeed is to throw yourself fully into the concern and get involved all the way, body, and soul.

Consider Technology

Email marketing campaigns can be successful, but only if they are executed properly. You will have to make those e-mails you send stand out from the crowd in a big way. The messages, the slogans, the bits that grab the attention, must be bigger and better than anyone else. Use graphics, Gif's, talking cartoons, use anything to get that message across, because if you don't, then your competitor will.

It is unbelievable that in the components of one smartphone is crammed more technology than allowed man to land on the moon. It is no wonder it is a non-profit's best friend. You have a captive audience. With instant social media feeds, you can drip-feed them information day after day on any topic you like.

Advertise Like a Business Would

Apart from the allure of the phone and its many possibilities, it is also important to make a list of different ways to advertise the fundraiser in the best way you can and certainly at the least cost to your new venture.

Consider these advertising outlets:

Local Radio Stations

Under the banner of the Federal Communications Commission (FCC), whose most recent figures show that there are approximately 15,500 US radio stations. Over 90% of the population listens to them at least for one hour per week. You do not have to be a math genius to realize the power they hold to influence the nation and its results for your charity concern. Most medium-sized towns have a radio station, as do most university and college campuses.

Let's not also forget the huge rise of internet-based radio stations, which most phones will be able to access. The potential for getting your cause across is enormous. You can produce a radio commercial yourself. All you need is a good script, a good speaker, and a point of common interest.

Local Publications

You should also utilize your local press and publications. If you live in a large enough community, you are bound to have a daily paper that covers the immediate area. Produce eye-catching adds, not only for the events that you are holding but for the local area to keep in touch with what you are doing. Hold interviews to tell people how much the last fundraiser made and keep those interested in your overall progress up to date. Draft a press release. This allows all manner of the press to access your information. If you are lucky, the editor may give you a weekly or monthly page or column in which to put your varied points across.

Public Access Television and Local TV Stations

Local TV should certainly be your port of call if you want to get your face seen. See the station manager and get them involved in what you are doing. They always need guests to fill particular programs. Establishing yourself as a minor local celebrity should fit that bill quite admirably.

Community Center and Programs

If you have a local community center, use it. Hold regular events and meetings there, get to know the people who run it, and show then that you can successfully bring in an interested, buying audience for the message you are advocating for. They will take a cut of your profits in building fees, but if you negotiate a sliding scale payment, this could be a long-term option. Also think, on any given day, they have offices that are unused, you could use them for committee meetings. Do not be afraid to ask, the only two answers you are going to get is yes or no.

Elicit Help from the Chamber of Commerce

There are approximately 7,800 Chambers of Commerce dotted throughout America. They should be your first port of call for all matters related to the running of your organization. Some of the larger ones have international affiliates with links to the major overseas charities. They will also lobby the government on any important issues you have directly relating to the day to day running of the business.

Utilize Local Influencers

Instagram, Snapchat, Facebook, the blog-o-sphere, and the whole of any social media platform is full of self-made influencers. Find those who would be likely to agree with your cause and call on them to help you get the word out, especially if that cause aligns with that influencers already-made brand image. For example, if you are starting a recycling initiative in your area, consider teaming up with a mom who blogs about being eco-friendly. You'd be amazed at the power of a shout out!

Be Focused

All activities and fundraising events are trying to reach a goal. Keep in mind the amount should be the net amount at the end minus expenses such as facilities, fees, and marketing costs. After creating a fundraising goal, it is easier to create a budget for expenses. Some expenses might include the cost of transportation, materials for different events, staff, invitations, space rental, and catering for events.

Keeping people involved in what you are trying to achieve is what matters. Think further than your short-term money goal. You are trying to sway the hearts and minds of your audience to help you champion your cause.

When it comes to choosing the type of fundraising event, consider the target audience. A fundraiser that is catered more towards parents of young children might have activities families would enjoy. Other fundraisers have activities and events for business professionals. Make sure to get enough help for all the events, whether through paid or volunteer staff. Have multiple methods of advertising for fundraising events.

"Service to others is the rent you pay for your room here on earth."
Mohammed Ali – Boxer, World Champion, Philanthropist, Political Activist

Online Presence

The most important function you will and most certainly need when you first start your charitable organization is your website. It is your shop window on the world to proclaim your mission, set out your stall, and above all, to tell everyone what it is you actually do.

This really is an essential tool, and you should spend considerable time and effort to develop it. It may be a job for a specialist design agency, or someone you know who has the technical know-how, but however you do it, it must look extremely professional.

Branding is Everything

Your image and brand name are undoubtedly important. Not only is it the first thing your clients will see if you make it memorable enough, but it is also the last thing they will remember.

Do a bit of homework here and surf the web for charities like yours. You will find how others do it, and certainly, within that research, you will find out what to do and what not to do.

Without a doubt, you need to be visible to future donors, volunteers, partners, and beneficiaries, so you'll need a clear and compelling brand. Consider your charity's tagline, the simple advertising grab point that people will recognize you by.

If you do not have a physical office or have not yet thought about a shop, it is essential that before you post the website that you arrange for a drop-off point for donations.

Willing shops, libraries, and community centers should all be approached as possible places, but nothing beats your own premises or your own shop!

The Mission Statement

Your mission statement gets to the heart of the matter. It outlines the aims and goals that you are looking to achieve, both short and long term. It is essential that these are as in-depth as you can make them. Great if you can have a time frame, even better if you have some immediate results to show from past efforts. It is laying out your stall and showing the world not only what you have to offer, but more importantly, how you are going to do it.

About Page/Defining Yourself

Gauge the likely impact of your work on the people or organizations it effects. Look inward. Do we practice what we preach? Do we implement and work under the dictates of the words respect, dignity, and excellence? Can we make a difference in our daily actions? If you cannot tick yes to those questions, then you are failing.

Do we make false promises to our donors and staff by failing to use the power of values? Look, if you do not have a passionate belief in empowering excluded people and to lead from the front by showing both staff and shareholders how we intend to do business, then when it comes to it, it really matters very little about what you do in the end.

Online Donations

Make sure you have a well thought out donations page with a listing of debit and credit options to suit everyone's needs. Remember to include the growing number of payment options, like PayPal or Google Wallet, and certainly make sure that you include your business address and company registration number. Make everything as transparent as can be so that the donor knows that this a bonafide giving experience. Be sure to file an SSL certificate so that you know the checkout system is safe. If you don't know what this means, ask your web developer or the hosting company. This is very important as it lets donors know that you have a safe and secure connection on the website, and it is perfectly safe to enter any personal information.

A secure and user-friendly website is now the way forward, especially if you do not have a physical address. Without it, and without your collective committee's imaginations going into its construction, launch, and regular maintenance, you are missing an essential marketing tool.

Open an Organization Shop

One way to generate recurring revenue would be to open a physical store. The proceeds from the items sold in this shop would go directly into your non-profit. Think about thrift stores, coffee shops, bakeries, and gift shops.

I know that the allure and interest in physical shops are dwindling, that the revenue streams are plummeting now that everything is available for purchase online. No matter how small the shop, it is still a physical presence that anyone can wander into and buy what you are selling.

Legalities

Obviously, you are going to have to register the charity, and its name with the relevant authorities as only registered non-profits can open shop premises, just as a business entity.

As a registered charity, you must provide detailed, publicly available information about your activities, finances, trustees, impact, and more. You may also want to set up a company, which then can be registered as a charity.

Within the articles of association, there must be a specific clause stating that no part of its assets shall benefit any people who are members, directors, officers, or agents (its principals). As well, the organizations must have a legal and charitable purpose. They may be created to support educational, religious, or charitable activities.

Be very aware that when you register with the IRS, there are various tax exemption forms. This may vary from state to state or even county to county. Checking out the legal side of how you set up the charity is essential, as is the understanding of your Federal and State rights. There is a list of things you can and cannot do, and you are under many of the same laws as for-profit organizations.

Be aware that in the US, there is a very heavy presence in the prevention of any misleading information or charitable fraud. Its remit falls under the legislator of all state governments to police and will certainly vary from state to state.

Create a budget for the shop, with likely income from sales and expenditure from overhead like rent, wages, repairs, bills, insurance, and supplies. Remember that 60-80% of a shop's income will go to running costs, such as rent and wages.

The shop will need to be safe, well lit, and accessible to those with disabilities and be placed in an area of good passing trade with more than ample parking. The public area will need shelves, railings, and a counter with a register, while the backroom will need storage and sorting facilities. Good security and surveillance equipment are also highly recommended.

If you do not have hands-on retail experience, then find someone who does. Hire someone who will be responsible for day-to-day activities such as, stock control, cash handling, customer service, and especially handling volunteers.

Day to Day Working

It is essential that you find volunteers. You will always need a minimum of two people working in the shop for safety, security, and stock processing.

Train your workforce so they know about your charity's aims, retail law, product safety, stock preparation, and spotting valuable goods, as well as issues like health & safety. They should be your ambassadors always, so they're keen to encourage donations, whether through chatting to the public or doing house-to-house collections. There are legal obligations involved in house-to-house collections – so check them out!

Be Up to Date

You need to keep the information on your website updated as regularly as you can. Certainly, you must make it as SEO friendly as possible. Search Engine Optimization is a technique used on the web for promoting keywords in a general search and as often as possible in order to connect with all the internet's available search engines. Include languages on your website and even paper communications that are used in your community's area. Leave no ethnic group out.

Keep the crowdfunding page regularly updated. Keep it alive by communicating frequently and keeping everyone posted on the progress. Really use your social media presence. After all, that's a completely free outlet.

It is also essential to be transparent. People want to know where their money goes. As your fundraising campaign progresses, you should develop two separate email lists, one for those who have not donated yet, and one for those that have donated and send them different types of updates throughout the campaign.

Online Help

Think back to the days before TV, the generations who can remember such a time are dying out at an alarming rate. Think back before we all had landline telephones. The eight-track, the cassette, and vinyl records are few and far between nowadays.

Generations have grown up knowing only the World Wide Web and the instant gratification of e-mail. Once upon a time, to research a topic, you had to spend hours, days, even weeks at various libraries just to track down the facts. Now, in a matter of seconds, you can have practically every fact and figure in front of you that you will ever want or need.

You would think it strange that someone would bother to set up a non-profit charity to save the pink-eared-Walla-Walla of New South Wales, and not know how to go about it. As with everything in life, do your homework and know what it needs and how you can help it. You must make the proposition as attractive as possible to your "customer."

Look at the cuteness factor. Try some photos of moms and their babies. People love to have something to either ooh, and aah over or pity. It appeals to both psychological needs equally, which is especially effective when you are trying to get money out of someone.

There are now so many opportunities and platforms in which to sell your charity. It all becomes rather baffling if you are not a marketing genius. You are not selling anything to the person you are aiming at, they are simply buying into the idea that you are showing them in the hope that it stirs their conscience enough to alleviate someone else's problem.

What's more, they do not even need to have cash in hand. It's all credit and debit cards, Apple Pay, PayPal, and invisible wallets bulging with money that no one has seen or ever will see. You can set up such a platform where you help charities run their fundraisers online by providing a user-friendly interface, technical support, and safe payment processing.

Charitable fundraising used to be simply taking in pennies or nickels and putting them in your teacher's collection plate, from which they would magically disappear into the ether to help the afflicted of whatever disaster or country they were needed for. Now, we are so overwhelmed with the simple act of giving that it has become more of a chore than a pleasure.

Your chore, as the owner and manager of a non-profit organization, is to overcome that dread of donation. You need not do it alone. Don't be afraid to hire or solicit help from like-minded professionals. You would be surprised how much someone is willing to donate their time to a cause they truly believe in.

Planning an Event

Insurance and planning for the unusual should form an integral part of your pre-event planning. Insurance is not always necessary, but it is advisable, especially where children are involved. Something will always go wrong.

We are now going to look at how to put on a local community event for your non-profit organization. I will try and cover all bases and eventualities. This section is designed to help you, and your guests enjoy themselves and give you, as the event planner and manager, maximum peace of mind.

Public events should be meticulously planned from the ground up and from start to finish, booking the venue, catering, and entertainment. A great deal of work goes on behind the scenes to make things run smoothly, but always be aware that things can and will go wrong, and that you certainly cannot plan for every eventuality.

Let's look at what you might be planning to do. Perhaps it is a fundraising event like a children's party, a sporting event, a disco party for teenagers, or even an event for the elderly. It might be a marquee on a green in the center of town or a local community building. You might be putting on an event just for close friends or for the whole community to attend. Whatever event you are holding, there are always risks attached.

Have you thought about the risks? If the party is outside, do you have a Plan B if the weather is bad? If you must go indoors, is the place suitable? How many people do you expect to attend? Is the venue big enough? If it's a sports-related activity, how is the ground fenced? Are you near a road? Will there be alcohol present, do you need a license? Are their first-aid kits available, and are their trained operatives in the vicinity?

Under the dictates of law in most countries on the face of the earth, you, as a charity and the events you put on under its auspices, have a 'duty of care' to protect the charity and not only its good name but also its assets and its resources; which of course includes your staff. Insurance companies will insure you. It is only when you file a claim that you will have a problem.

If you are hiring out a venue, even just a church hall or a community center, you are responsible for the insurance. Some may be stringent and insist on a certain percentage of cover. Holding an outdoor event, you should also get cover for that, especially if you have hired anything from horses, a local celebrity, to a troupe of dancing elephants.

To claim any of the expenses through your insurance company, all events that have been canceled or abandoned must have been deemed as beyond your control, an act of God, fire, or flood. Expenses covered range from recouping the cost of printing tickets, publicity, venue hire, purchase of perishables like foodstuffs that have a limited shelf life, hire of any ancillary equipment, lighting rigs, generators, and relocating or rescheduling the canceled event.

Establishing an Entity as a Charity

You must examine if the charity you are going to form is actually needed. You have to do your research to make sure you are not wasting your own and everybody else's time. You should determine if any other organization is doing what you do and, if so, how you could do it better. Make sure you never compete with another charity chasing the same money for the same cause. One of you is going to lose!

You have to cast your net as wide as possible. How many people are going to use the service? Do a random phone poll or a mass email. The results you get back will help you determine how good your idea actually is. You should also study trends such as what the likelihood is of your donation flow increasing, and how many clients you could aim for after one to three years of operation.

Be sure of what you want to achieve even before you have begun to act. The stated objectives of your purpose for your existence should all be enshrined in your mission statement. Your aims should be a broad batch or goals that you wish to achieve, and how you are going to achieve them. You may decide that it is through a biannual fundraiser or raising a specific financial amount over a fixed period of time. By organizing your objectives into a precise form of action, charities can more effectively serve the groups they set out to help in the first place. Whatever the cause is, the charity's focus should always be concentrated on the fulfillment of those aims and striving to achieve them.

It is often viewed that sometimes raising awareness about an issue is a crucial part of fixing the issue itself. Charities may aim to raise awareness in their mission statements, but also may enact policies to reach specific those objectives. For example, a charity that aims to raise awareness about a pet overpopulation problem might want to provide outreach to students in a local school with the objective of compelling families to spay or neuter their pets.

Charities can raise awareness in many ways, such as holding educational events, writing monthly newsletters, or starting T-shirt or bumper sticker campaigns, for instance.

You cannot do this on your own. Bond with a likeminded group of people and form a trustee committee. One of you should be voted chairman, one secretary, and one treasurer. Make sure you settle all disputes/resolutions/decisions by vote and certainly never leave the table before settling all disagreements, it only leads to friction.

Make your charity's name unique. Think of the World Wildlife Fund compared to the Wisconsin Women's Force. They seem different until you break them down to their initials. Everyone donates to the former just because of its uppercase letters, WWF. It is known worldwide and is instantly recognizable. Unfortunately, the same cannot be said about the latter. So, pick a name that stands out and fits the cause you are fighting for.

Register your charity's name with the federal registrar. It then operates as a non-profit organization under state and federal law as tax-exempt status. They fall under code 5013c of the Internal Revenue Service's code. As a recognized status, you will be able to raise money for your chosen cause helping people but must not engage in any political activities while doing so.

Non-Profit organizations are regulated at two levels. The first is on the federal level by the IRS, which grants exemption status to those eligible. The IRS also regulates to ensure they serve the public good, and all their activities are legal and above board.

At the state level, it is the Attorney General who keeps an eye on the organization and its fundraising activities within their designated state border.

One of your most important functions is how you will target the public and how they will recognize you instantly and register what you do by the logo alone. Bold colors work best while keeping with your objectives. Remember to trademark the name and logo under your own company copyright imprint.

Everything you do in life is on a learning curve. There is an arc of experience, recognition, and then acceptance of the facts that stand before you. Everybody and everything changes, and as you grow, both you, your attitude towards what you do, and what your charity achieves, will change as well.

Starting a project fresh, from the get-go and the ground up, you will make all the inevitable mistakes. You will make the wrong decisions or implement the wrong strategies. Wrong or right, you will carve out a path in pursuit of your goal and realize not to do it again.

If you do not have the idea of a total and have not grasped its importance, how can you impart that to someone else? Your own commitment should be as strong. It should be stronger than any of your colleagues. Always lead from the front, delegate wisely, and make sure before you make that final decision that you have thought it through thoroughly.

Charities have a terrible habit of spawning other charities. So, it is no surprise that a lot of likeminded organizations are joining together to form larger and bigger fundraising companies. That is all well and good, but you have to establish a set of guidelines right at the start of any discussion. The first two things that need to be thrashed out are trust and transparency.

Trust, because if your CEO and Committee do not trust the partner organization's CEO and Committee, then what is the point! Things are not going to happen overnight, as trust is always built on shared values and principles. It is simply not enough to have common goals and an identical mission statement; you may have dramatically different approaches to the same problem or issue. It's about how you work things out and agree on a solution that makes all the difference. Be transparent, be open, be honest, and be fair in your joint approach to each other

You are also going to encounter problems in joint reputations. Make sure at the outset that you both have impeccable standards. If there are skeletons anywhere that they have all been outed from the closets and you start your new venture with a clean bill of health. Finally, you have to be sure that the impact of the partnership is worth all the effort. It is not the short-term goals you should be worrying about, but the longer-term implications of you working with another charity. It is not about raising immediate revenue streams, it's about your longer-term commitment to shared goals and community interests.

In all the busyness of doing, a simple thank you to those who have supported your cause is often overlooked. You must always remember that you are building a relationship for now and on into the future. You are certainly always looking for ways to deepen that relationship. If it is a smaller concern, say a church, school, or community fundraising, you should try to contact all donors personally. By speaking to them, you will find out what they thought about the idea, slipping in the request of how they would like to be contacted in the future.

You should be trying to deepen the bond between you and the donor, telling them how much they are appreciated and valued. I am sure you will be surprised by the response that you receive. Everyone likes the hands-on touch, the feeling that you took the time to contact them and thank them personally for their contribution. Supporter engagement and public trust have never been more important. Now is the time to reassess the power of a simple thank you. Supporters want to hear from you again, and it will also give you a better picture of their varied needs.

The impact of a positive call is further reaching than just the feel-good factor of the message. It also helps you identify and build the knowledge and understanding of your supporters. By a simply stated set of questions, you will identify vulnerable donors, which can enable the charity to adapt the way it communicates with them in the future.

Hiring a Publicity Company

Should we use a specialist fundraising company or do it ourselves?

The simple answer to that question is that the only way you are really going to learn the ropes is by doing it yourself. If that is too big a leap right at this moment, then there are other options you can consider.

There is a certain satisfaction in achieving something on your own terms. It gives you pride in your own self-worth. As a growing organization, you will know each other strengths and weaknesses and know which one of you can handle which bit of the fundraiser the best.

Now, that is, of course, just fine if it is something small and manageable. You will make mistakes, but more importantly, you will learn. Consider it on the job training, so there is nothing better.

Event organizers have sprung up in the wake of charity growth in the past 20 years. They are the unseen hands behind some of the largest charity events in the country. They can organize anything from cycle runs, marathons, treks, and triathlons, with flair, expertise, and above all, safety. They have teams who can think of the measures that you have not, so if you have the idea, they have the solution on how to best promote it.

Most have templates for bespoke events or tailor something from the ground up, leaving you secure in the knowledge that they are as committed to raising as much money for the cause as possible. It is probably why they have a revolving list of clients who return to use their talents time and time again.

How to Find the Right Event Planner

Below are just a few tips on searching out the right charity events organizer.

Check out the Company you are considering on the web and review their previous clients. You will immediately discover if you are a good fit. It will also throw up a list of those who found their services lacking.

Always check the terms and conditions before you sign anything. Get your lawyer to pick through the contract to see there are no hidden fees or penalties, should anything go wrong on both sides, of course.

Check around and ask questions of an organization that has used their services before, and no, it's not sneaky. You are putting your event into their hands; you want to ensure that they have a good record and that all the problems they may encounter are ticked off from the list in your own mind.

Ensure that the company is in compliance with the Better Business Bureau. Are previous clients satisfied with the company?

This will take you an hour or two to find out at most, and this valuable information will most certainly save you heartache should things go wrong. It all about safeguarding yourself and your charity's interests.

Pros of Hiring a Pro

One of the many positives about using event companies is that they will always look at the bigger picture, the one that will bring in the most revenue. These events can either take place in your own town or county, nationwide or for the more exotic, overseas.

For the privilege, they usually ask the fundraiser to pay an upfront entry fee or at least contribute to the cost of the challenge on top of monies raised on behalf of the charity. If the challenge event is not wholly organized by the charity or its volunteers, there are a couple of ways that companies are involved.

> (a) A company offers an event directly, and members of the public can take part to fundraise for a cause

> (b) The charity contracts a travel company to book a tour such as an Everest expedition or Kilimanjaro trip and asks its volunteers/supporters to take part

Event organizers are only for the events that you do not have the skills to do yourself. Just think of the skill needed to put on a cycle race from New York to Washington, D.C, or San Francisco to Los Angeles. Currently, the logistics are just too big for you to handle, but there is no harm in dreaming.

Plan a Lottery or Raffle

There are a lot of reasons people run lotteries. For example, they may wish to collect money for good causes or to help their local sports center buy equipment for special needs clients. Always be aware that lotteries are, in fact, a form of gambling with strict regulations and safeguards that are in place.

Each country has libraries full of statutes on gambling, which are most certainly upgraded each year and heavily governed. In the US, each state will have a different set of rules which may differ from the Federal ones, so please check individual regulations wherever you may be. You may even be regulated by a central gambling commission whose rules must be strictly adhered to.

What Makes a Lottery?

A lottery is a basic kind of gambling infused with three ingredients.

- You have to pay to enter the game

- There is always at least ONE prize

- Prizes are won purely by chance

A lottery is basically a raffle like the one that you would find in your Church Hall, Community Center, or social club any day of the week. An array of numbers and perhaps colored tickets all drawn randomly; those numbers are drawn, each winning a prize.

Another example is a sweepstakes, where you draw a series of random numbers or tickets. Sometimes these are used in conjunction with a sporting event, perhaps a horse race, or a car race, or something similar.

It is also important to stress that the charity is totally transparent, for every dollar raised, you must have a paper trail to show where it went. Always remember you are in the non-profit game. If you are big enough, you have salaries and legitimate expenses.

The tickets for a lottery on a specific date must show the name of the charity, the ticket price, the name, registered address of the organization, and the date of the drawing along with a unique number.

With a little imagination and effort, lotteries will for little outlay on the organizers part, can bring in a considerable return. You are appealing to people's basest nature. Everyone is interested because everyone likes to win. You are appealing to people's dreams, no matter the lottery winnings. It is the dreams of those who buy the ticket that the money or prize may give them a better quality of life.

One only has to look at the success of televised lotteries all over the global, yes anyone who buys a ticket hopes to win, and of course, anyone can, as long as you are lucky and have the correct sequence of numbers on that particular day.

Other Local Fundraising Ideas

Nothing in life is static. We are all always in a state of forward movement, whether we like it or not. We build relationships both strong and weak with our supporters, listening to both their needs and understanding their ambitions, trying all the while to match them with the right fundraising need, at the right time.

Community fundraisers must have a handle on building powerful relationships with those they deal with, by putting their volunteers at the very heart of what they do. Being business savvy would certainly help, but personal skills and an endless abundance of enthusiasm for what they are doing is essential.

As the leader of a community fundraising team, you are at the center of a time of great change. Legislation and the future impact of everything being digital, charities as a whole are losing revenue daily. Every charity on the planet is always looking for ways to replace lost income. The prospect of community fundraising allows opportunities to extend yourself and engage with minorities and varied groups that are spread across your communities, and certainly how you can build long-lasting relationships with your supporters.

To be a fundraiser – I mean the head of the team – you have to be confident enough that you have the knowledge, interpersonal skills, and confident personality to be able to clear the way for all the problems that may arise.

I would really like to look at how various sections of the community consider the business of fundraising, from the view of the local community, the primary dictates of the Christian community, and, of course, the business sector, corporate, and individual. Make no doubts about it; they are all after the same aim, which is to raise as much money for their individual projects and shine like a thousand stars in heaven.

So, let us keep it simple here, you have a short-term aim to possibly a longer-term problem, it matters little if you are in a rural or a suburban setting. Each has its own problems - corn and its subsistence or people and their forwardness. Each is a problem, and each has an outcome, no matter the way they play out.

Local fundraising is all about getting the community where you live involved in what you are doing. The more friends or contacts you have, the more opportunities you have. You need to develop and manage a team with the appropriate skills, knowing what future relationships need to be put in place.

Bear in mind the knowledge needed to get a foothold in a now saturated and crowded market that is any kind of fundraising. Be open and build mutually beneficial and productive relationships that carry you through.

Always remember that the power of what you do lies in its heart, in the power of stories. Stories have since time immemorial have always connected people together; they are a powerful tool that should be used at every opportunity, and for the best effect. You have a charity, so you engage people in the area with it.

Let's look at something simple, you have a community sports field that needs upgrading. You are desperately needing to upgrade the changing rooms, revamp the seating, and put in some simple catering facilities. Tell people the history of it, invent characters who speak directly to donors about it, and promote it where and whenever you can - newsletters, online media, broadcasts on local TV, and the radio.

I have listed below certain tried and tested ways of raising money for your community charity. By the nature of writing, it is certainly not comprehensive enough. But you would give me no points if I did all the work for you. Nothing in life is exhaustive. Nothing is comprehensive, apart from the research that you do to satisfy and justify your own soul.

Selling Vintage Clothing

Strangely enough, vintage wear has been growing in popularity during recent years. Any era from pre-WWII until the '90s shows no signs of slowing down – especially old worn jeans like Levi's and Wrangler. You can combine them in your store with an online display, maybe even selling banner ads on special items of interest.

You just have to spend time yourself going to flea-markets, thrift stores, and yard sales to see what is out there. Look out for clearance sales and special online sales. Both are good ways to stock up your own store if you can get it cheap and sell it for a hefty profit.

Craft Sales

One of the old chestnuts of the non-profit trade is the classic craft sale. The options are endless. Say you know a potter, sell their wares, and put the profit to charity, a woodturner to sell their output and do the same. You can organize and hold a community craft sale, selling booth space, and entry fees. After paying for the facility, staff, and advertising, your profit should be gold!

Car Wash

Hold a limited-time event and get your neighbors to lend a hand. Think about doing it on a regular basis. Use teenagers supervised by an adult and make an event out of it. Perhaps a local school could turn their parking lot over for your use once a month. Another good place is to approach gas stations, especially one that is situated on a busy road and may not have a car wash facility of their own.

Go to the Dogs

Well, here we have some options here. We know about organizing dog washes to raise funds for a good cause, but you can take it a step further. You could open a doggie day-care center. Pet owners are becoming increasingly aware that it is not healthy to leave their pets at home all day alone. They become morose and depressed, which, in the end, leads to destructive behavior.

Dogs, like people, are social creatures and need contact with people and other dogs to become well-behaved and confident individuals. Drop them off in the morning, pick them up in the evening. Ideal, of course, if you have a lot of time and space.

Socialization is certainly the most important thing puppies need in their early stages of development. A puppy who is not socialized is a problem, aggression towards other dogs being only one of many problems you will encounter with them. Consider offering dog walking services. Take dogs for a long walk, ideal for wearing then out thoroughly for a long nap later.

Host Special Nights

It does not matter if you are a large or small community, you will be made up of different ethnic groups, so how about a Burns' Night supper for Scottish people, or a St. Patrick's Day supper for the Irish. Consider any other supper celebration for all those many diversifications that live amongst you as you can think of.

Community Yard Sale

A yard sale is a sure-fire way to bring in revenue. You can use a school parking lot, a communal space in front of the church, even open stalls inside the church. Scour the community far and wide for anything that is saleable. Everyone who has a basement and an attic knows what gems are hidden away in both. Everything is resalable, and everything has a value, your team just has to find it.

Babysitting

Parents are always looking for reliable childcare. If you have space and folks eager to babysit, then this is a great fundraiser that you can turn into a small and regular business. Though nights are a popular time that parents are looking for babysitters, think outside the box. Try offering babysitting services so that parents can shop for the holidays, for example. That they can hunt for presents for surprises for their little ones. The more diversified and qualified you are, the better for your business.

These are just some of the many fundraising opportunities that are available to you. You and your committee need to draw up a comprehensive list and go for it.

Faith-Based Fundraising Ideas

Here we engage a fundamentally different idea to the structure of fundraising. Everything that goes through that structure must have the Christian Mantra at its heart. You are not there to make money for money's sake, but for its benefit for the aid in helping someone else.

Donors will always support a cause that is important to them, so it is your job to sell the idea to them. You have identified a need – in the church, community, or a broader basis – now convince them how they can make a difference. It is how you communicate the urgency of that need and, in the end, honor the donor's intent that makes all the difference. Oh, and thanking them for their support will do little harm either.

A church is made up of the sum of its parts, namely, the congregation. It is vitally important that you impart to them the nature of the common goal and the importance that you reach it. Work as a team from the start to create a statement of church fundraising policy. Create a list of priorities. Start a meeting with a blank sheet of paper and answer some simple questions.

- What is our objective?
- Can we achieve it right from the get-go?
- Is this idea for the good of the whole?
- Does this idea uphold our values?

It is better that you and your committee argue at the beginning and get everything out into the open, rather than leaving things to simmer, brew, boil and then explode. It is much better to get everyone's feelings out at the start rather than having to face that wrath later on.

What makes a non-profit church? The statement below has been taken directly for the current IRS website so that there is no confusion.

> *Churches must meet specific requirements in order to obtain and maintain tax-exempt status; these are outlined in "IRS Publication 1828: Tax Guide for Churches and Religious Organizations." This guide outlines activities allowed and not allowed by churches under the 501(c)(3) designation.*

It was in 1980 that a recognized 14-part test was determined to recognize a standard assessment as to whether or not a religious organization could be considered a charity for the purposes of IRS rules.

These parts include:

- A distinct legal entity
- A recognized creed and form of worship
- A definite and distinct ecclesiastical government
- A formal code of doctrine and discipline
- A distinct religious history
- A membership not associated with any other church or denomination
- A complete organization of ordained ministers ministering to their congregations
- Ordained ministers selected after completed prescribed courses of study
- Literature of its own
- Established places of worship
- Regular congregations
- Regular religious services
- Sunday schools for the religious instruction of the young
- Schools for the preparation of its ministers

The most important factor in deciding status is that a religious charity must have an established congregation and an organized central ministry. A common belief and purpose that hold together the individuals of the congregation are respected in so much as they join together in regular religious worship in a centralized position. The IRS does not recognize that even though the church may broadcast their services to an outside source via radio, those listeners do not count. It is the physical presence of the congregation that matters.

It has been said that it is easier to hold on to a donor than get a new one. So many opportunities are lost because people handle money differently. Some prefer online giving, some writing checks, some paying over the phone, and some in-person cash donations.

The US has always been dominated by the church ethos. Thousands of churches, thousands of communities, and certainly thousands upon thousands of well-meaning, right-thinking people are the glue that holds the fabric of the nation together. They bond together in an effort to reach and pursue that common good for all that can and may benefit from its healing hands.

The church community wields a huge stick in a small space, they can also do big things if they are given a solid purpose and remit to do it. They have become a base plate for any number of community events, gatherings, and good causes. Always remember you are fighting with all the other churches and small community groups for the slice of that pie. You must want that slice more than your competitors. That is no mean fete, especially if your church is isolated, and your congregation is small. These are certainly problems, yet, not insurmountable ones, but you must want to solve the many problems they pose.

You probably have to proceed outside of Sunday meetings, whether it be morning, afternoon, or evening. You have delivered a sermon on whatever and certainly left a message of some import, leave it at that, your congregation is still chewing over what you have said earlier, they probably have no desire to hear you sound off about yet another problem that neither they nor you can control.

Talk about the fundraiser in your newsletter, at coffee mornings at social gatherings, and slowly ease people toward your goal. When you finally tackle the subject that is close to your heart, you hit it head-on; it is not such a big issue. After all, you know your church and your congregation, and you should be able to play them off as suits you and the parish that you work for.

We talked about websites, social media, and the mainstream media themselves. You will soon become adept at how to use them to your best advantage. You should, of course, be encouraging your congregation to be doing the same, time after time, after time.

It is essential that you keep everyone informed, no matter what you are doing, good or bad. You have social media, you have your dedicated website, Facebook, Twitter; all those possibilities are endless. Produce videos, podcasts, and pictures because most of them cost nothing at all with all the free content online. It goes without saying that anyone with a working tablet, an iPhone, or a working laptop has only the limits of their imagination to stop them from creating. All it takes is a little pinch of flair and imagination.

Always remember that your $5 donor can turn into a $10 donor; it is up to you, once you have her on the hook, if you reel her in, or simply choose to let her wriggle off the line and slip away to help someone else. She has given you a certain amount of information – e-mail, website, address, phone number – to use for the benefit of the cause.

Have your like-minded friends put your collective heads together – think out of the box, push the collective envelope, and have a far better idea than these outdated clichés I have just been using.

Prayer Meetings

You can hold prayer meetings at the homes of members and collect funds. You can also visit homes with your group and offer prayers to residents.

Pop-Up Café

Open a pop-up café in your church and run it on a weekly basis; of course, if you have the volunteers, you can open more regularly, ideally daily.

Spiritual Concerts

Hold a concert with your church choir and singers at some venue. You can charge tickets for the show.

Donation Boxes

Keep donation boxes at schools, colleges, and stores where people can drop change. This is one of the good ways to raise funds without much effort7d.

Bake Sale

Ask members to bake their favorite dish and sell reasonable portions with some margins.

Auctions

Get church members to donate stuff and hold an auction. The money collected goes for church fundraising.

Carol Singing

Singing carols is an old Christmas favorite. Either go door to door or hold a ticketed event in your local town square or community center; hot coffee, mulled wine, and mince-pies, of course, are optional extras.

Work-a-thon

Work within the community, such as litter clearing, getting rid of things that have been discarded, weeding gardens, painting, and cleaning. Helping the elderly or performing tasks for disabled people in your community, or even repairs around the church itself. People who donate to this fundraiser know they're supporting church programs and get a chance to give much-needed services to elderly or disabled friends, family, and community members. It's a wonderful fundraising tactic that raises money and gets church members involved in community outreach.

Dinner Event

Dinners are a staple for many churches. But what about offering dinner on one of the other nights of the week? You can raise money and give families a night off from cooking and doing dishes. Encouraging diners to buy their tickets in advance can help you keep costs to a minimum, and it gives parents and families a chance to take a night off from cooking and doing dishes. Consider allowing people to eat at the church or take their food to go so people can plan their week accordingly.

Crowdfunding

Crowdfunding or crowdsourcing is a means by which a person, group of people, or, indeed, as a charity can pitch their idea by posting it on a crowdfunding website. You cut out a bank as the crowd refers to the likeminded people or organizations who are willing to support that idea. These are broken down into different ways of funding:

- Investment-based crowdfunding – where someone invests in your idea, and they receive a stake in it (shares)
- Loan-based crowdfunding. Where money is lent in return for a set interest rate. Generally called P2P – Peer to Peer, or P2B- Peer to Business
- Donation-based crowdfunding. Donations given to a charity are rewarded by something in return
- Reward-based crowdfunding. You give money in return for a reward linked to the cause you are supporting. In the respects of charity crowdfunding, you have to be quite specific in your aims.

Email Fundraising

You will reach a far wider audience from your desk and your laptop than you ever can by doing it face to face. Email marketing is nothing new, you just have to follow a few simple rules, or perhaps invent some new ones. First, beware of spamming, people do not like it and will simply delete the message without bothering to read it. Start with your own congregation first, then ask for referrals, and then ask those referrals for referrals, and so on.

In a very short time, you should have a substantial list of people who you must keep in touch with regularly. Be direct and talk to them as if you were talking to them in person; give them a story about the work you do, the explanation for the mission, and why you need their money so badly. Do not labor the point. Get in and get out as quick as possible using direct language and firm words.

The only way to raise money over e-mail is to ask for it. Don't try to hide the purpose of your e-mail. Be honest, get to the point, and ask for a donation. Make sure once you have made a positive contact, you stay in touch at least every couple of months, making sure you are not always asking for money as it all becomes boring. Keep your donor interested and informed about the project.

Like all fundraising, it is a case of if you can think of an idea, you can put into place the idea. Bear in mind that you should always be flexible in your approach towards your committee and your donors alike, one drives what you wish to achieve, while the other one feeds it. Treat them both with equal respect and give them both thanks – remember that your volunteers are unpaid, and your donors do not have to support you, and you are the cement that holds the whole operation together. Do not let them down.

School Fundraising Ideas

Children in different age groups will have different fundraising ideas. A kindergarten fundraiser differs from an elementary school fundraiser, as does a High School fundraiser, which is going to present a completely different set of problems than a University fundraiser. All are headaches which only force you to come up with new solutions to cater to all of them. Everything seems to have been done before, or perhaps you are lacking in either ideas or motivation.

Many teachers use their own funds out of pocket to pay for supplies and materials in their classrooms. Federal, state and local funding is falling woefully short of what is actually required to provide students with the tools they need to excel academically, socially, and emotionally.

Something always needs fixing as things are forever broken, that's why schools need to purchase upgrades to computers, general technology, playground equipment and perhaps special needs items, as well as providing teachers with adequate funding so that they can carry out their job as efficiently as they can. Unfortunately, fundraisers are now more than likely to be for the benefit of the educational institution rather than the wider world.

It is rather sad that in a recent study of elementary school teachers across the US, the lack of books was the biggest problem. One teacher said it this way:

> *As an elementary school, teaching students how to read is fundamental to what we do. The best way for them to learn is to get as many books as you can in their hands. Thanks to our fundraising efforts, we provide students with relevant, grade-level titles to push them to become the very best readers they can be.*

So, go form a small committee, brainstorm a set of proposals, and then book an appointment with the school principal. Take one of your committee members along as a back-up and present your case.

It would be good, with the help of a laptop and a printer, that you put your ideas down in the form of a firm proposal for everyone to see. Treat this as you would treat any normal business idea, the more professional you appear, the better the chance you will have of exciting those you present to.

Schools all around the world need extra funding and are very receptive to parent input. It would be great if your idea centered around a gap in their support market, auxiliary, or supply teachers or even in classroom help – especially for the youngest members of the class or for those with special needs.

But no matter what stage they are at, you must remember that they are still children, so you have to make, no matter the activity, as much fun as it can be. Tailor the fundraiser to the children's level.

Kindergarten/Pre-school

They are at the beginning of their journey, so keep it simple. Little ones love to sing, so perhaps you could host a karaoke party. Get the parents/grandparents into the classroom to have fun with nursery rhymes. Sell a class calendar made with photos that the children take. Planting a school garden is a good way of teaching about the joys of nature. Set up a team whose job it is to tend and water the vegetables, then bag and sell them to the parents.

If you want to keep it seasonal, what about Breakfast with Santa? Keep it modest, rope in a male member of the staff, dress him appropriately, give out presents, and prepared breakfast for an entrance fee. Plan a summer or spring carnival with the usual round of games and entertainment with prizes attached.

Elementary Schools

They are still small children, but they certainly have far more sophisticated needs than the younger ones. Some ideas for this age group include:

- Raffle tickets
- Bake sales
- Spaghetti supper
- School picture days
- Walk-a-Thon
- Partnering with local restaurants for "spirit night" fundraising
- Cookie dough sales
- Brochure gift item sales
- Vote on a teacher/staff to get a pie in the face; the teacher who raises the most money in donations gets pied!

High School

(Which includes Middle/Secondary school students.) With this age group, they now believe themselves to be grown up, so you have to give them their heads and be a little more sophisticated with your approach. Hosting a school dance as a fundraiser is an idea that can often be overlooked yet can turn out to be very effective, where you can combine raffles, best dressed, couple of the night, etc. into an amalgam where students of all ages can have fun.

- Homework pass purchases
- No uniform day incentives
- Chocolate sales
- Car wash
- Candy grams on holidays (Valentine's Day, Christmas)

University

This is a different consideration altogether. All Universities have extensive charity provisions raising millions of $ for every cause known. You are also dealing with the next generation of business and political leaders, so you must steer them in a particular way. Raise something inter-team, inter-college, inter-university, and challenge your rivals at something, anything, be it football, chess, tennis; it does not matter as long as it is testing you both and you have a good time in the doing of it and raise some money.

What about designating someone who is going to break every rule in the rule book for a day, to skip classes, to barge into dinner with the dean of the faculty, walk consistently on the grass that is specifically not allowed – use your imagination and let your naughtiness flow.

Of course, there are far more sensible ideas, like the usual round of fashion/charity shows and general ideas of how to raise money, although you who are the future of your nation, should be able to come up with a whole catalog of something different.

The only thing that is going to hold you back in any of this is you and your imagination. As long as it is safe, enjoyable, fun, and profitable, there really is nothing that you cannot do. Even the most challenging things are not a problem as long as they are well planned, well prepared, and well supervised, then there should be no problems.

Corporate Fundraising Ideas

About 4 years ago, seven of my friends and I sailed a small boat across the North Sea from Edinburgh to Stavanger in Norway for charity. We spent six days out in the open, hardly sleeping, not washing, meager rations, sickness in wild seas, complete and utter exhaustion at the end of just short of 600 kilometers. We raised about $12,000 dollars for the charity. It was one of the best things I have ever done!

Corporations were once in line for themselves, suddenly they have discovered a new St George, larger than the dragons that they once battled. They have arisen out of the fire and show that they care. Being number one is no longer enough. Being number one must show that you care big time. The very nature of the corporate fundraiser is a huge public relations exercise, a profile raiser, and a definite promotion of your personal profile.

It is generally accepted in corporate circles that donating to charities is something that they must do and have to be seen to be doing. They want to give something back and do good, although that once simple mission statement has altered recently. The emphasis has changed, and there is an awareness that a need has arisen to tackle not only the broader arc of society but also things that directly affect their own business practices.

They have been forced to look at how their own companies deal with their suppliers and their circumstances and how they can use the philanthropic act to alleviate the problems they encounter. Years ago, we cared only about what we bought, not where it was grown, or who made it. Now we aware of appalling wage, working, and living conditions in the third world where these goods are either made or grown.

This has led to partnerships between large and small businesses and charities to not only carry out philanthropic acts but also to change living and working conditions for the better for those in most need. Corporations want one thing out of giving, and that is to maximize publicity for their organization, but if they can help a good cause, then all the better.

It boils down to positive publicity and someone saying something good about your product. If you can harness it to some outside need, then all the better. Most large companies now employ the services of advertising agencies, or they may even hire a specialist charity or fundraising professional to do fundraising work for them.

Look at any major sporting event, and you will see corporate banners hanging, advertising, or promoting something. In a lot of cases, they are sponsoring the club or sport itself, not a bad way to get potential customers on your side. You like the club or sport; they like the club or sport. It becomes a visual form of subtle psychology in which everyone wins.

In the workplace, it is how you utilize the staff you have to get the result you want. Never forget, it is also about them. Organizing charity drives fosters team spirit within the group, but always remember that they have individual lives away from work, so their time is precious. Use it and them wisely.

Get your employees involved from the very beginning. Have them suggest ideas and pick the most popular. As you are all adults, it could be anything as diverse as:

- a wine tasting night
- gambling night held on company premises
- casual dress day

- swear jar
- fashion show
- company picnic
- sell branded T-shirts
- Corporate Cookbook
- Direct Mail Fundraiser
- Host a 5K run/walk

It could be any number of ideas to get your employees motivated and involved.

Seeing a company's altruism will be recognized and noted by the buyers of the brand. Non-profits rely heavily on social media and the exposure to the media in general, so by letting its customers know what fundraising drives they are having and the financial results of them.

Form a committee to handle these events. Motivate that committee, remembering that it is an amalgam of many different ideas. That makes not only a good team but a good fundraiser as well.

It does not matter if you are a large thriving company, a struggling company, a new startup, or a sole proprietor, you can all make a difference when it comes to the act of charity. You have the personnel and the resources to make that vital difference to the cause you have chosen to fight for.

Not only do you have compliant staff, but you also have a network of suppliers, their suppliers, and, in fact, their suppliers as well to draw on. Each are prospective clients for the cause, a field that you can furrow for now and develop for the future.

In the workplace, be it a hair salon that employs 4 people, an engineering firm that employs 50, or a branch of a corporate faction that employs 5,000, you can all make a difference as long as you work together for that common goal.

More and more companies are raising awareness of the problems outside their own sphere. It is not a bad thing. In some cases, it makes the workforce view the world in a different way, and certainly makes them aware of their place in it. It does not matter what you do if it makes a difference, and you care about it. You can sit and say, but it is only when you do that the whole thing comes together.

One man trying to build a pyramid is bound to fail. 50 men trying to build a pyramid with the correct instruction, motivation, and direction can build it in no time. Being a manager, you know the strengths and weaknesses of your staff in the workplace, yet, you may not know them as the individuals they are.

On a different course, perhaps you could set up a temporary store in the foyer where for a limited time. You could draw all these people together to paint pictures, write poems, bake cakes, and produce jam for the benefit of your chosen cause.

Say you are a corporation with several regional offices. You could advertise the fact that you are doing these fundraisers. You should never underestimate the power of the internet. You can advertise, you can sell, you can trade, you can do anything and everything to raise money for your non-profit once it stops being company time and begins being your time.

Charity is an invisible quantity, you are giving, but you are not in any way receiving in return. It becomes an entity that you cannot feel, touch, taste, nor see; it is unrecognizable to the human eye and the human soul, yet ultimately it affects everyone. If you want a return for those who are investing in your idea, then offering a return for their money is a pretty good way to go.

Above all, be daring and look for the idea that no one has thought about or the angle that you are all missing. Be creative, be safe, and above all, remember you are a business, and any charity ideas cannot get in the way of day to day business, your clients and company always come; first, the rest is all just fun.

"You have not lived today until you have done something for someone who can never repay you."
John Bunyan, English Christian Writer, and Preacher

Fundraising in General

By now you would have thought we had exhausted the whole topic of fundraising, but hang on a minute, there really are still some important things to say. There is plenty more to the topic before we reach our conclusion.

Passion is a pretty exhausting emotion, and the passion for running a non-profit charity really must be all-consuming. You certainly cannot grow it from the ground up without donations from individuals, organizations, and help from governmental agencies. Those contributions must add up to a substantial amount over time if you are to remain afloat.

It is, of course, down to you and your committee to secure those donations. This is easier said than done. Approaching your board, any one of the members might have a whole bag full of conflicting ideas and a very difficult time in deciding what approach to follow. You have a goal to raise a large number of funds, which is perfectly attainable with the appropriate research and the right resources.

Sometimes you have to bend your own ethics in order to move your charity forward. For example, say you are a charity that runs a hospice for terminally ill smokers. Approach cigarette manufacturers, growers of tobacco, or any ancillary smoking-related product producers. Now that is not a bad taste, it is more common sense as both are linked together in a state of reverse psychology, or cause and effect. You should always be on the lookout for large, well-funded companies and corporations whose goals fit in with yours and target them for larger donations, rather than casting your net around for many single individuals who may give smaller amounts.

Make sure that you are continually updating your events and do not use the same ideas year after year. Be inventive and be creative. People get fed up if you keep giving them the same set of fundraisers and will go in search of something new. Enthusiasm fatigue and burnout really do happen. One, because people are fed up with the same old thing and two because they are trying so hard for the cause that their attention span and compassion meters waver. They lose the buzz of what they were doing. Try to hold a few small events across the calendar to generate interest and bring in a little money. Combine with several major casual events relating to the group's cause that will perhaps bring in a lot more.

If you are trying to raise a lot of money at once, do a little research first. Find out locally and nationally which businesses are currently making substantial profits and concentrate your efforts on those. It stands to reason; you have a greater chance of success with people who actually have surplus cash that they can spread around than someone who is in borderline profit. Always be aware of the possibilities that are around you. Rethink, redraw, and then discard any strategies that you feel are not working and then implement new ones.

If you are up for it and have the chutzpah to give it a go, government agencies are a good source for large funding projects. Charities of all sizes have the right to pitch to them but be aware that your pitch had better be outstanding. There is a lot of fierce competition. Your idea must be on the grand scale, one that helps not only the community but also one that government agencies can oversee and take responsibility for. These range from local employment non-profits who concentrate on finding employment for those in need of benefit from state or city agencies. One that focuses on oversees affairs would apply to a federal agency, and, of course, anything to do with medical research would talk to the Center for Disease Control.

Why People Do Not Donate

We have already been through the reasons people donate to a fundraising drive, but what if they don't donate. Why would they not want to donate to a cause that means so much to you? Are people not interested in what you are saying or what you are doing? Are the goals you have set a little too modest so that there is a lack of urgency in your staff and volunteers?

It is up to you to convince people that what you are doing is for the right reasons, and what they do does make a difference. People shy away from contributing to any sort of fundraiser because they don't actually know what their money is being used for. Could it simply be going into someone's bottomless pocket?

People, in general, have had enough of putting their hands in their pockets for so-called good causes. Here are some common excuses for not donating:

- Look, it is hard enough to feed my own family, why should I subsidize someone else's?

- Everything is costing more each day; I do not have anything to spare for fundraisers!

- I am really not interested, nothing that is happening at the moment excites me; it is always just someone else with their hand open. It means nothing.

- Hey, your timing really is off. It is the end of the month, it's coming on Christmas, my car needs new tires. Come back next month.

- My money won't do any good. It will make no difference.

- I don't really trust charities.

- The people who need it most, it will all disappear in overhead costs.

- It just makes those people dependent.

- I volunteer, I do not have to donate.

- I send my old clothes for recycling, is that not enough?

These are all valid responses. You, as the fundraiser, have to keep hitting the mark and come up with new and innovative ways to raise funds for the cause.

"To ease another's heartache is to forget one's own."
Abraham Lincoln, US President

Conclusion

In a book of this size, you can only scratch the surface of the many ways that you can fundraise for your cause. There are literally thousands of ideas from thousands of websites that will fire up your imagination.

Fundraising is not a static exercise. It is about invention and then reinvention. If you can think it, then you can do it. It is all about constructive thought and then constructive criticism. Thrash things out at your regular committee meetings. Decide what is right and wrong for you. Talk over what is right for the image of the charity, the type of fundraisers you will do, and, most certainly, the type of fun raisers you will not do.

Whatever message you put across and whatever you are raising money for, make it people centric. In whatever you do, tell a story, paint a mental picture, leave people with a lasting impression of what you are aiming to achieve.

Always remember that you are asking for people's money. You must make a rock-solid case so that they feel committed enough by the points you have raised to give it to you.

Remember to treat the individual donor as just that - an individual! Yes, you are appealing to the many, but you must concentrate on the few. Engage your donor as if they were a friend, and that you are only picking up a conversation you had with them the last time you met. It is the human touch that makes all the difference. Certainly, assuring them that their donation, no matter how large or small, made a difference.

It does not matter if your donor is giving you a dollar or their life savings. It does not matter if it is the old lady 2 blocks away that wants to fund your refuge for local cats, or the local convenience store who wants to give you their sell-by-date food. It does not matter if it's your local church looking to fund the replacement of pipes from their beloved 19th-century organ or the enormous corporation who has decided to back your next large-scale project. Treat them all with the same respect and dignity.

Always remember it is about building relationships. Treat everyone as you would like to be treated.

Be unique in your approach. Think of something that has not been done before.

Donating to charity has come a long way in the past 200 years. Computers and software make the whole art of giving for the charity and its implementation so much easier for the donor. Everyone is on a donor database so that they can be targeted again and again. Major corporations have a Development Department looking for the next big idea and solution to the latest set of problems.

No one book can ever hope to give you all the information you may need on the subject of non-profit organizations, their set-up, and day to day running. Therefore, I urge you to do as much homework before you set out so that you are ready for all eventualities.

No matter the path you go down, or certainly how you promote your charity, handle its daily challenges in stride. Manage your team well, whether they be full time or part-time staff or even your intermittent volunteers. You have a huge task on your hands, competing in a highly driven and competitive yet shrinking market. You have a very long and hard road ahead of you. I can only wish you well in all your endeavors for the future.

Resources

I have waded through a great number of websites – only a fraction of which are listed here – to put this book together. Of course, there is an endless stream of information, help, and guidance on how to seed, tend, and grow all sorts of non-profit organizations.

As in all things, do a program of thorough research before you begin to make decisions.

https://www.paypal.com/fundraiser/112574644767835624/

https://charity.lovetoknow.com/What_Percentage_of_Donations_Go_to_Charity

https://www.americanfund.info/

https://www.theguardian.com/voluntary-sector-network/2014/feb/26/how-to-measure-impact-small-charity

https://www.christianaid.org.uk/

https://www.worldvision.org.uk/who-we-are/about-world-vision/

https://www.transparenthands.org/list-of-top-15-charity-organizations-in-usa/

https://www.usa.gov/donate-to-charity

https://greatergood.com/clicktogive/ggc/about-us

https://www.thegivingmachine.co.uk/fundraising-ideas/

https://www.signupgenius.com/nonprofit/50-creative-and-easy-fundraising-ideas.cfm

https://www.classy.org/blog/25-quick-fundraising-ideas-for-nonprofits-and-charity/

https://www.transparenthands.org/list-of-top-8-charitable-organizations-in-united-states-of-america/

https://www.hg.org/nonprofit-organizations.html

https://www.answers.com/Q/Are_there_any_charities_in_the_US_that_you_can_donate_cancelled_stamps_to

https://piponline.org.uk/get-involved/schools-fundraising-for-us/

https://doublethedonation.com/tips/fundraising-ideas-for-schools/

https://donorbox.org/nonprofit-blog/school-fundraising-ideas/

https://thirdspacelearning.com/blog/school-fundraising-ideas-for-primary-schools-25-genius-ideas/

https://charity.lovetoknow.com/What_Percentage_of_Donations_Go_to_Charity

https://money.howstuffworks.com/economics/volunteer/starting-a-charity/rules-charities-follow.htm

https://www.charityexcellence.co.uk/Home/About

www.ingramcontent.com/pod-product-compliance
Lightning Source LLC
Chambersburg PA
CBHW071414210526
45465CB00001B/386